Tenement Press 15, MMXXIV
ISBN 978-1-917304-01-6

Six Sermons for Bob Dylan
Lucy Sante

What the world needs now are these conjured sermons from the always brilliant mind of Lucy Sante. In these rollicking and clarifying exhortations, she urges us to find the good and the God in everyone. We look inward, see how we have faltered, and discover our humanity. What is so refreshing is the call to love all of us: the fallen, the fools, the forgotten.
 —Dana Spiotta

This beautiful book will appeal to sinners and the saved alike.
 —Scott Bunn, *Aquarium Drunkard*

(An introduction.), Lucy Sante		13
I	Hypocrisy	23
II	Virtue	29
III	Gluttony	35
IV	Temperance	41
V	Justice	47
VI	Prudence	53

'Now pick up your bed — and walk'   59
(An afterword.), Greil Marcus

In August 2016 I received an email from Jeff Rosen, Bob Dylan's majordomo. I had been getting occasional writing assignments from Bob through Jeff for years, and they were extremely various: speeches, press kits, prefaces, a Buick commercial. Now he explained that he and Bob had been discussing a film project, to focus on his 'Gospel Years,' 1979–1980. They had some great footage—not the rather stiff performances intended for an unmade TV special, but the rougher takes made for pick-ups. Bob had the thought that he'd like to interrupt the footage with sermons delivered by an actor. Would I consider writing the sermons?

I gulped, but I said yes. What did I know about sermons? Barring the occasional funeral I hadn't been to church since age thirteen, and what I could recall of the priests of my past was not exactly inspiring. I searched sermons online but found mostly dull plodding slabs of Midwestern Mainstream-Protestant reasonableness. I searched my bookshelves for anything relevant and came up with Perry Miller's 1956 anthology *The American Puritans*, but their elegant plain seventeenth-century Dissenter prose did not suit the music. I also found *Saved: The Gospel Speeches* (1990), transcriptions of the sermons Bob had actually issued from the stage in those years, edited by Clinton Heylin and published in Raymond Foye's palm-sized Hanuman editions. They weren't prose at all, but spontaneous exhortations and rambling homilies, full of doom and repentance, blood and thunder. I checked with Jeff, but no, Bob did not want those as a stylistic model.

Finally I realised what I should have known in the first place if it weren't for my print bias: my sources had to be recorded sermons. After all, I had dozens on my iPod (RIP): Rev. J.M. Gates, Rev. D.C. Rice, Rev. A.W. Nix. These were Black, mostly Southern preachers of the 1920s and '30s, whose recorded sermons, often unaccompanied, handily outsold the blues issued on the same labels. I had never seriously listened to them one after the other. I remembered some of the more sensational bits, such as Rev. Gates's 'Death Might Be Your Santa Claus,' or his 'Atlanta gets her styles from New York, and New York gets her styles from Paris, and Paris gets her styles from Hell!'

But when I listened to the sermons one after another, the thing that struck me was their earnestness, their neighbourliness. The secret of their success was that the preachers seemed to be addressing specific people, and that included you. I imagined Southern Black families brought north to cold factory towns, finding in the sermons the warmth of home. The language they used was everyday; educated but not off-putting, familial but with no concessions to slang. The examples they employed were concrete: urban to solicit immediate awareness, rural to reawaken early moral instruction. And they were grounded in the rhythms and imagery of the King James Bible. Never having done more than browse through it, I had to give myself a crash course.

Left to Right—Rev. Matthew G. Carter, Dr. Martin Luther King, Jr., and Rev. Deual C. Rice / Union Baptist Church of Montclair (Montclair, NJ), 1966.

That is why I relish unexpected assignments: they force me out of myself. I found myself inhabiting a young, energetic African Methodist Episcopal minister in an urban parish: Augusta, Jackson, Memphis, Indianapolis, Washington DC; I pictured the Black middle class as represented by the advertisements for Paramount Records in the *Chicago Defender*. Good-looking, well-dressed young professionals exhibiting mild reactions and taking responsible stances—even if they are occasionally chased by jealous lovers or wind up in the jail house. I played fast and loose with the historical setting—alluding for example to jake-leg drinkers (consumers of a Jamaican ginger extract that caused paralysis of the lower limbs) from the 1920s, but also, unavoidably, to fast food from more recent times. Bob had assigned me six topics: Hypocrisy, Virtue, Gluttony, Temperance, Justice, Prudence. I took them seriously and surprised myself with the plausibility of my preacher's moral reasoning. Somehow, even while staunchly unreligious (I don't call myself an atheist because we really don't know, do we?), I had inhabited religion, and not derisively. Am I the devil citing scripture?

Lucy Sante, MMXXIV

Six Sermons for Bob Dylan

Let us have wine and women, mirth and laughter,
Sermons and soda-water the day after.
　　—Lord Byron, *Don Juan*
　　　(CANTO 2, ST. 178.)

1 Hypocrisy

You will find my text in the Book of Matthew—Chapter Seven, Verse Five—where the apostle quotes King Jesus saying, '*Thou hypocrite! First cast the beam out of thine own eye, and then thou shalt see clearly to cast the mote out of thy brother's eye.*'

Brothers and sisters, dearly beloved, you are the most pious congregation in the county, maybe even in the entire state. There is no one like you for praying to almighty God, for raising your voices in song, for swaying and dancing and making merry in Jesus' name. You give generously to the collection basket every Sunday. You come here in your finest clothes to do God proud. You open your Bibles every night to read a passage of scripture to meditate upon before you go to sleep. You are truly blessed by the Father.

And yet I have seen you, brothers and sisters, I have seen and heard you as you walk down the streets of our city. I have seen you pass by the magdalenes on Third Street, and by the pool players on Fourth Street, and by the jake leg drinkers and the hurdy-gurdy players on Fifth Street, and I have heard your mutterings and your imprecations. I have heard a certain sister say of those fallen women that they are filth that should be swept off the streets of our town. I have seen a brother laugh as a poor old rummy broke a leg trying to run away from his demons. I have seen pious folk step around the body of a poor man lying on the curb, not knowing whether he was alive or dead and maybe in urgent need of medical care. I have not looked for such things. I have only come upon them in the course of my daily business, and I know that what I saw and heard were not out of the ordinary.

At the same time, I have heard tales. I do not invite gossip, which is the devil's work, and I do not give it credence. And yet, in our small city, tales do slither around, and follow the breeze from porch to porch, and creep in through the scullery window. There may be no basis to the stories that a certain brother of this congregation frequently visits a woman in the next town, who has borne his child as she has borne those of several of her other admirers. It may be absolutely false to think that a certain sister whom we all know and love has an intimate acquaintance with the demon codeine. There may be no reason to believe that a couple of brothers here owe such large debts to a certain fancy man in a slouch hat that they have taken out second mortgages on the homes where they live with their wives and children —debts that have mounted because they are always certain that they can fan those cards and roll those bones and beat the odds that are jiggered by the man in the hat.

I'm sure there is no basis to any of these idle tales, and that they are contrived by evildoers in order to besmirch the good names of our pious brethren. But wouldn't you agree, brothers and sisters, that sometimes where there is smoke there is also fire? That maybe those stories contain a germ of truth? We need not concern ourselves with the details, and we certainly should not be looking around the room to see which of our members might fit those descriptions. That is for God and the Devil to decide. Instead, what you and I should be doing, brothers and sisters, is to look long and steady into our own hearts. Because if we examine our hearts patiently and without prejudice, we will find worms crawling there. We will find snakes and toads. We will find many things we would not want our wives or husbands to know, nor our neighbours, and especially not our children. And therefore, I ask you, church, are any of us in a fit position to judge those fallen men and women on the side streets of our town? Because if you can look into your heart and still decide that you are better than they are, I submit that you are a hypocrite! That sin will be counted in addition to your other sins on the day of God's wrath! Remove that four-by-four piece of lumber that is in the way of your sight!

11   Virtue

I take my reading today from Proverbs, Chapter Ten and Verse Nine. '*He who walketh upright do so surely, but he that perverteth his ways shall be known.*'

I believe it was one of German philosophers who once wrote, 'Out of the crooked timber of humanity, no straight thing was ever made.' He was not wrong, that German philosopher, because we are all sinners in the eyes of the Lord, we are all that crooked timber. Every one of us has our share of iniquities and vices. But he was not right, either. I'm sure all of you have had the experience, when you set out to build a new hen house or corn crib, that you order some boards from the sawmill and, the way these things go, some of the boards are a little bit crooked. Or else they have bumps and ridges in them. Not necessarily the sawmill's fault—trees bend as they grow. But what do you do? You can't send them back, and you can't afford to throw them away. You have to use them. So you take out your plane, you spit on your hands, and you have at it. For hours sometimes. Just planing away until your hands are sore and your arms are sore and your back hurts. But then, at the end of it, you have a piece of wood you can use in that one spot where you need it. You can put together your hen house, and after you've given it a coat of paint, even you can't remember which one was the crooked board.

That is the way God's grace works on our imperfect souls. If we are willing, God will take us and straighten us out. God will exercise his blessed elbow grease on our crooked hides, on our sinful selves, and he will make us upright! But you have to be willing. God will not invest his labour on just anybody, on just any drunkard or liar or cheater who wants to pass his bent carcass through the narrow gates of paradise. You have to be willing, and you have to work with God. For God to make you straight you have to pray and fast and sing and do good works. You have to love all the other sinners and not judge them or talk behind your hand. You have to share your blessings with others, even though they be drunkards or liars or cheaters. If you can do all that, the Lord will make you straight. You can walk down the street at high noon, and everyone will say, 'There goes an upright man.'

As I mentioned, we are all crooked, we are all sinners. But some of us are more crooked than others. Some of us keep council with the devil and become more crooked still. That becomes known, too. I don't mean those poor unfortunates who cannot drag themselves out of whatever mire of drinking and gambling keeps them prisoners. There is hope for them if it doesn't come too late. I mean those highly respectable people, who dress conservatively and keep a charming house, who are well-spoken and highly educated—who may even attend church, and raise their voices in song, and contribute to the steeple fund and the choir fund and the missionary fund—and then go home and cheat widows and orphans out of their meagre inheritances. Who take a cut from the bootlegger when he comes through town with a supply of bottled poison. Who rig the scales in their place of business so that every purchase weighs a little bit less than what it says on the bag. Who threaten their tenants when they are late with the rent but don't fix the broken windows or the hole in the roof. Who tell tales on others and ruin their reputations, just for fun. These people walk around, seemingly upright, sure to give everyone the impression that they are among the righteous. But though they may fool you or me for a while, God knows the truth. God can see right through the fine manners and the sweet talk. God knows that they are so bent that they will never pass through those gates on high. And sooner or later everyone else will know it, too. You cannot hide from God! Your sins will find you out!

III Gluttony

This morning, I take my reading from First Corinthians, Chapter Three, Verses Sixteen and Seventeen. '*Know you not that you are the temple of God, and that the spirit of God dwelleth in you? If any man defile the temple of God, him shall God destroy, for the temple of God is holy, and you are that temple.*'

    It has come to my attention that some of the members of this congregation have been seen skulking around downtown, bearing greasy paper bags in one hand and in the other one of those cups that are just about big enough to stand umbrellas in. You know who you are, brothers and sisters. I will not shame you by looking in your direction. I know how good that all tastes, that fried chicken and that hamburger meat with cheese and those fried potatoes and that sugary sweet soda water. Those foods have given all of us sustenance at times, many times that we have not been able to taste the vegetables that we have plucked from the soil with our own hands, the yams and greens and cabbage and runner beans that are nature's bounty given to us by God. It happens that very often we are in the big town, we are travelling, and packed meals from home can only go so far, and we see a bright illuminated sign and it draws us in when we are hungry. And we purchase that food and that drink and it satisfies us. It sends a message from our belly to our mind that tells us we are happy. Far be it from me to condemn that simple pleasure.

    But what happens, brothers and sisters, when a few hours later—maybe in a different neighbourhood—we see another sign beckon to us from across the road, and before we know it we are hungry again? What happens when we capitulate to that momentary craving and go in and have another meal? We are happy for an hour—more or less—and then our belly starts to complain. We may have to let out our belt a few inches, we may even feel a little sick. Our bodies are telling us that we must ease off, that we've gone too far and we best not let it occur again. But what happens, brothers and sisters, when our children are running around and yelling, and we forgot to go to the grocery store, and maybe there's something wrong with the stove, and we have a headache and shin splints, and we just cannot face cooking dinner for our family, so we take them to the shiny place down the road where they sell that chicken and those potatoes and those sugary soft drinks? Nothing wrong with that, you'll say, happens to all of us. Yes, but what if it happens the next night when you are tired, and the night after that when you've had a hard day at work, and the night after that when you are just feeling lazy? Very soon you and your children will not fit into your clothes. Your children will become loud and wild from the sugar, if they don't instead become soft and limp from the food. Sooner or later all of you will get sick.

Brothers and sisters, as the Bible says, your body is the temple of God, the temple of the Holy Spirit. When you fill your body with fat and sugar and starch and salt you are defiling the temple! You are insulting God who gave you your body! When God gave you your body, he also gave you instructions on how to take care of it, which is to say that you received those instructions from your mother, who got them from her mother, who got them from her mother in turn. Your foremothers did not go to the shiny store and buy their dinner in a greasy bag. God gave you the soil and the plants that grow in that soil that provide wholesome nutrition for your body and your mind and your soul. When you replace the fruits of nature's bounty with that sweet, fat, salty, dripping mess made in a factory somewhere by men who charge you a dollar for every nickel they spend on that imitation food, you are spitting in the temple! You are drawing devil's faces on its walls! You are cursing God just as you are cursing yourself!

'It is written. MY HOUSE SHALL BE CALLED THE HOUSE OF PRAYER'
The CHRISTIAN MISSION

IV Temperance

Brothers and sisters, I read to you today from Proverbs, Chapter Twenty, Verse One. *'Wine is a mocker, strong drink is raging, and whosoever is deceived thereby is not wise.'*

I feel that I should not have to tell you about the evils of strong drink, brothers and sisters. You have the evidence all around you in the streets of our town. You see brothers emerge from bars and clubs at all hours, their clothes dishevelled and their breath foul, their feet tangled up in their steps. You see women with lipstick grotesquely smeared across their faces, fallen on the curb outside the cocktail lounge. You see young boys lurching around in vacant lots, smashing their empty bottles of cheap wine against the sides of the buildings. If you travel a little farther downtown, you see things that were once men sleeping in doorways, huddled around trashcan fires, the filthy rags they wear hardly enough to cover them, begging nickels from strangers, with no place to go, no family that will recognise them, no joy or even sorrow, no link to the world, nothing at all in their life but that next drink.

And meanwhile everywhere you go you see and hear enticements. You see the jolly bartender polishing a glass, suggesting you enjoy a nice cold beer. You see the slick businessmen around a table hoisting glasses of spirits telling you that you can be just as slick as they are if you'll just buy a bottle of Old Soak. Every magazine you open, every billboard you pass, the hoardings at the baseball diamond, the stair risers going up to the elevated train, the merry coloured streamers in the window of the liquor store—everywhere you look there is a sign telling you to drink! To drink the abomination that reduces men and women to crawling filth! When sometimes you can look right underneath that sign and see with your own eyes what wine and strong drink had wrought!

Brothers and sisters, I would wager that every one of us has a brother or a sister, an uncle or a cousin or a nephew who is in the grip of demon alcohol. Sometimes we hear about their activities from a wife or a child who has escaped their murderous rages and come to us for shelter. Sometimes we hear about it from the police when we have to go bail them out from jail where they have been incarcerated for public drunkenness or public indecency or vagrancy or malicious damage. Sometimes we hear about it from the coroner when they have dropped dead and need to be identified. Sometimes they themselves come to us, full of promises to reform, beseeching us the loan of a few dollars to get them back on their feet—and then we do not see them again for months, and when we do it is likely to be on the sidewalk at our feet. Sometimes these people are never spoken of in our homes, perhaps because they have disgraced the family name, or maybe because they have disappeared into a world of soup kitchens and hobo jungles.

But sometimes, just sometimes, that brother or sister, that uncle or cousin or nephew will come to us because they have truly had enough of that life, that lifeless life, that death-in-life. And then, with the help of almighty God, we can help them. We can restore their bodies with healthful food and pure water and fresh air, and we can restore their souls with the word of the gospel. It is rare and it is hard, brothers and sisters, but no drunkard is truly beyond redemption if he wants it badly enough. Because of this we must love the drunkard. We must love the drunkard even if he seems beyond hope, even if he disgraces the family name, even if he has compiled a police record two inches thick. For even as Jesus healed the sick and caused the blind to see, so he can bring drunkards to sobriety and to the love of God.

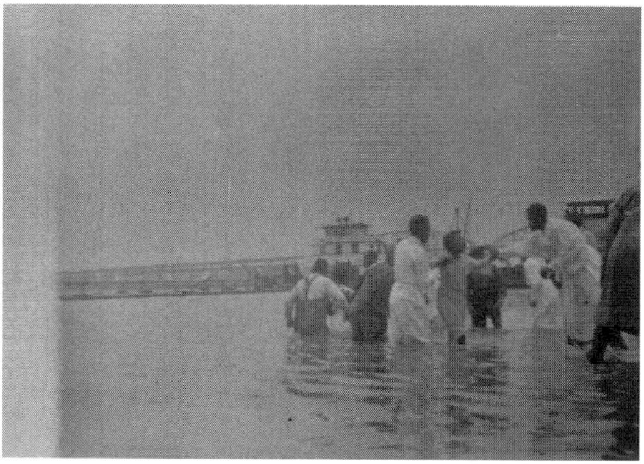

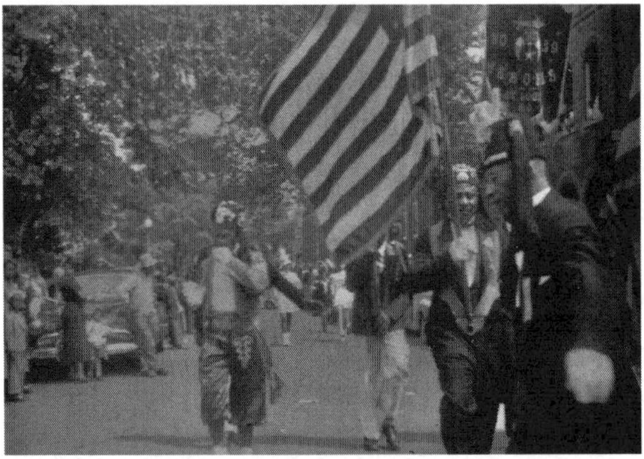

v   Justice

My text is the epistle of James, the Second Chapter, the Second Verse. *'For if there come into your assembly a man with a gold ring, in goodly apparel, and there come in also a poor man in vile rags. And you shall have respect to him that weareth the fine clothing, and you say to him, "Sit you there in a good place," and say to the poor, "You stand over there," or "Sit down at my feet," have you not become a judge with evil intent?'*

That rich man, you've seen him in town, you've seen him step from the bank to his fine automobile, you've seen him come through the door with a beautiful daughter on his arm, you've seen him through the window of the eating place tipping back his cup of wine and laughing, and you've seen his servants laughing when he laughs, and when he frowns they frown. You've seen the picture of the rich man in the newspaper, wearing his beautiful clothes, maybe bragging on his racehorses, his private yacht, his many houses so that he doesn't have to sleep in the same bed but once a month, and maybe you've thought to yourself that that rich man must be beloved of God. Because why else would God give him all that gold and all that finery? He must be beloved of God the way he is beloved of all the people—all the people who open doors for him and brush the dust from his coat and laugh when he laughs. Yes, that rich man must surely be meriting of God's love.

And then you see that poor man. You see that poor man walking slowly down the road, just shuffling along, with all the time in the world. The poor man is in no hurry because he has no place to be. You see that poor man looking at the shop windows, looking at every one of the goods on display there, but he doesn't go in. No, he doesn't go into the store. Instead, he sneaks around the back to where they keep the trash cans, where they throw the food that's become too old to sell, the fruit that's gone brown, the cheese that's grown mould. And what does he do, that poor man? He stands there and eats that food that is not good enough to sell, the food that you or I would turn up our noses at. And maybe you think to yourself that God hates that man—hates him as much as the store manager does, who when he sees that poor man eating that old food chases him away with a broom handle. God must surely hate that man, otherwise he would not have made him suffer.

But what if I were to tell you that the rich man has put mothers with suckling babes out of their houses when they were late on their rent? What if I told you that the rich man has raised prices on medicine needed by the sick so that many die from want of the money to pay for it? What if I told you that the rich man you admire so much has made his fortune from cheating other men out of their savings? That he has invited them to give him their money so that he could make it grow, but instead he has taken that money and put it into his own pocket, and laughed? And what if I told you that the poor man was an upright Christian man, with a family and a position—until the day when he entrusted the rich man with his savings? Now what do you think God thinks of those two men? Which of those two men do you think will be rich in the kingdom of heaven, and which one a beggar behind the gates of hell? So when you invite the rich man to take the best seat and tell the poor man to go stand in the corner, are you doing God's work, or the devil's? For I say unto you that justice is not always served on this earth. Sometimes the wicked are rewarded and the virtuous are made to suffer. That may happen in this life, but it will not happen in the next. For it is at the judgment that God will administer justice. And the things that are valued on earth will turn to ashes, and purity and goodness will become more precious than pearls. And the poor man will ride in glory, while the rich man will weep, but no one will weep along with him, for he will be alone in the darkness.

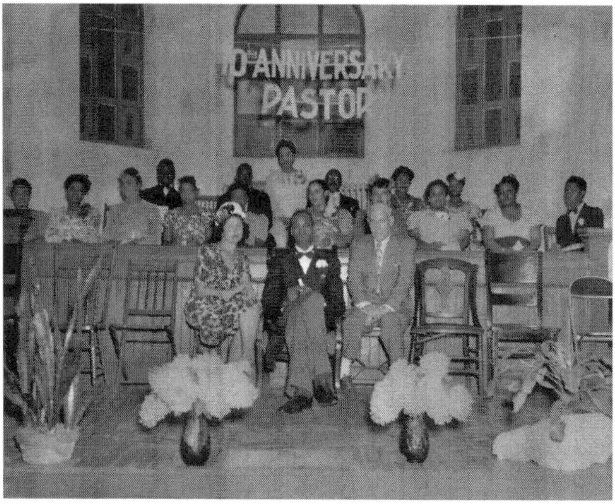
ANNIVERSARY
PASTOR

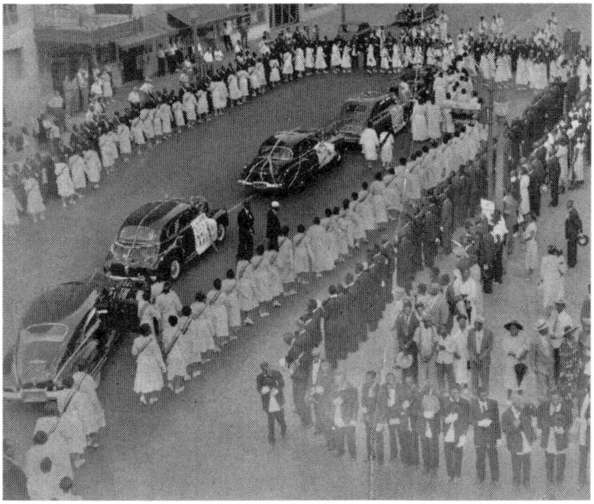

VI   Prudence

Today I am reading to you from the book of Proverbs, Chapter Thirteen, Verse Sixteen. *'Every prudent man dealeth from knowledge, but a fool layeth open his folly.'*

This verse is very much like the old proverb that advises, 'Fools rush in, where wise men fear to tread.' Fools are brave, brothers and sisters, and the world would be much poorer without them. When people first explored new lands, fools helped them tell which plants were poisonous by eating them and getting sick. Fools were the ones who found out that lions and tigers are dangerous. The first man to fly was a fool. He flew high, but not very far. A fool explored the floor of the ocean. It's a shame he didn't come back to tell us about it. The true discoverer of electricity was a fool who stood under a tree during a thunderstorm. Fools are always the first to rush into battle.

We all know fools. We meet them at the depot and at the market. They get on the wrong train, wander away from their baggages, get themselves swindled by confidence men. They are constantly paying too much for this and complaining they are being robbed for that, because they cannot do figures, although they think they can. If we were not good Christians, brothers and sisters, we could be making big money selling shiny rubbish to fools. Despite the fact that we are good Christians we now and then enjoy a laugh at the expense of a fool. It's not so much that fools are lacking in brains—we ourselves may not rank among the great minds of our time. Rather it's that they are so sure of themselves, so eager to jump into any new adventure without making sure there will be a floor for them to land on. And sometimes fools succeed. They go over the falls and come back alive. They climb the mountain without proper equipment and somehow survive. When that happens, we forget that they are fools and call them heroes.

Does that mean that heroes are fools? After all, you would pretty much have to be a fool to rush into the burning house, wouldn't you? But what if there was a little girl crying at the window? Maybe then you would find yourself with the child in your arms, rushing out again, not really sure how you did that. What happened is that you became a fool for a minute. Even if you were the wisest man in the county you might decide, on rare occasions, to become a fool for a minute. There's a difference in kinds of foolishness, of course. A fool rushes into the path of a moving train to save his hat, but it is a different kind of fool who rushes into the path of a moving train to save an old lady who has tripped and fallen. We should all have the opportunity to be that kind of fool at least once in our lives.

But most of the time we prefer to be prudent. We look both ways before crossing the street. We sniff the meat to make sure it hasn't gone bad. When we walk into an abandoned house, we test to make sure the floor will support our weight. We don't walk into the bull's yard, but go around it. If a salesman calls at our door to make us an offer on life insurance or an automobile or a set of encyclopedias and the price seems too good to be true, we read the contract carefully. We prepare for winter, we prepare for hard times, we prepare for the visit of our in-laws, we prepare when the creek starts to rise, we prepare when the newspaper tells us that the price of dried beans is about to go up sharply. And if we are living right, we prepare for our passage into the next world. We read the manual, which is scripture. We take out insurance, which is good work. We trim down our luggage, by cutting out sin and vice. We speak to the manager, who is almighty God. And even if we are fools in every other part of our lives, but we prepare for heaven, then we are the wisest of all.

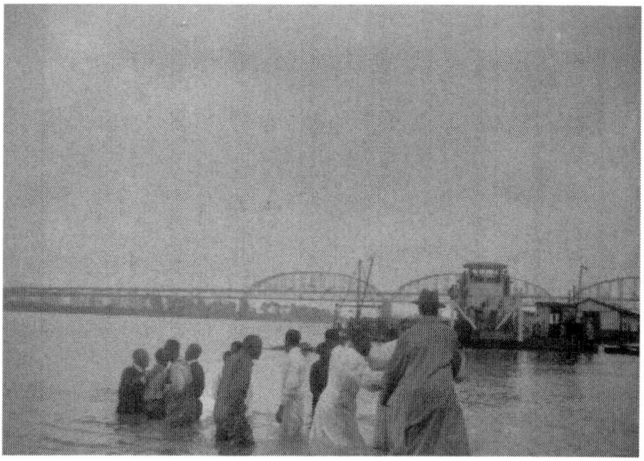

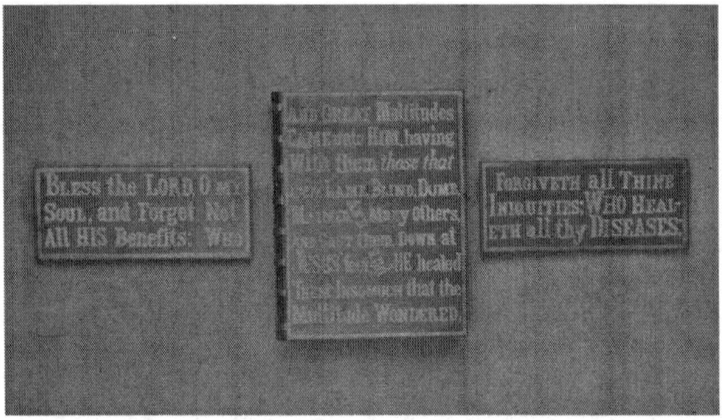

'Now pick up your bed—and walk'
Greil Marcus

In his appearance in *Trouble No More*, Michael Shannon, dressed in a dark suit, walks out of shadows toward the camera. The camera follows his feet up several stairs to a platform. When the camera pulls back, we see this is a preacher, at the podium of his elegant, high-ceilinged church, a vast window of stained glass behind him, with Christ on the cross at the centre.

Shannon must have seemed like a natural. The highpoints of his career as an actor are when his already heavy, craggy, dark face darkens even more, and you begin to think he, whoever this person behind the role may be, has never smiled in his life. Whether he's playing the madman as truth teller, a young man just out of the asylum and on his way back in *Revolutionary Road* in 2008, or if he's the sinner as avenging angel, in a dozen roles, but getting more dank and corrupted year by year as a Bureau of Prohibition agent in *Boardwalk Empire* from 2010 to 2014, he will always be the man with the bad news. The first words out of his mouth as he begins to speak Lucy Sante's first sermon: 'Thou hypocrites!'

And whether he is prophesising damnation, speaking reassuringly, shouting or condemning, one strain is constant: there is not a hint of humour, or even a laugh, mere amusement, over the iniquity of the human condition. And it becomes tiresome. Before Shannon's preacher has reached Sante's 'Justice' or 'Prudence' you may have made your way quietly out of the church.

This is not what you find when you read the full texts of the sermons Sante wrote in 2017. As she says in her introduction here, she's following in the footsteps of the likes of the Rev. J.M. Gates of Atlanta (1884–1945), and his 1926 sermon, 'Death May Be Your Santa Claus,' which as a 78 on the Okeh label sold scores of thousands of copies and was played by black families over and over all through the year.

*

While we think on the 25th of December, we are expecting a great day. But on that day it is said that Jesus was born, but we celebrate Christmas wrong. From the way I look at this matter, shooting fireworks, cursing, and dancing. Raising all other kinds of sand.

Ah, but death may be your Santa Claus. Those of you who are speaking to the little folks and telling them that Santa Claus coming to see 'em, and the little boys telling mother and father, "Tell old Santa to bring me a little pistol," that same little gun may be death in that boy's home. Death may be his Santa Claus.

That little old girl is saying to mother and to father, "Tell old Santa Claus to bring me a little deck of cards that I may play five-up in the park." While the child play, death may be her Santa Claus.

Those of you that has prepared to take your automobiles and now fixing up the old tires, an' getting your spares ready and overhauling your automobile, death may be your Santa Claus.

You is decorating your room and getting ready for all night dance, death may be your Santa Claus.

Death is on your track and gonna overtake you after a while. Death may be your Santa Claus. Oh man, oh woman, oh boy, oh girl, if I were you, I would be worrying this morning and would search deep down in my heart. For God I live and for God I'll die. If I were you, I'd turn around this morning. Death may be your Santa Claus. Death been on your track ever since you were born, ever since you been in the world. Death winked at your mother three times before you was born into this sinnin' world. Death is gonna bring you down after while, after while; Death may be your Santa Claus.

*

REV. J. M. GATES
Pastor Mt. Calvary Baptist Church, Rockdale Park,
2nd and 4th Sundays

Piney Grove, Buck Head, (Atlanta)
1st and 3rd Sundays

President of the New Hope B. Y. P. U. Convention of Georgia
and one of the best Revivalists in Georgia

Residence 424 Fraser Street,   Atlanta, Georgia

Inside all the doom, there's delight. There's a sense of fun in composition. There's the preacher's sense that as a man of God he's got to catch the ear and hold it, so he's also a stand-up comic. He takes pleasure, and gives pleasure, in word play, in the set-up, in the turnaround, offering you a thing of apparent value and then pulling the string. There's a lightness here, the same lightness you find in Sante's sermons as they sing on the page. In her 'Hypocrisy' with her 'brothers and sisters, I have seen and heard you as you walk down the streets of our city. I have seen you pass by the Magdalenes on Third Street, and by the pool players on Fourth Street, and by the jake-leg drinkers and the hurdy-gurdy players on Fifth Street'—and you can feel the congregation like yourself saying, *No, don't stop there! What's on Sixth Street?* Or in 'Temperance,' Sante as much a movie set designer as a moraliser,

> You see brothers emerge from bars and clubs at all hours, their clothes dishevelled and their breath foul, their feet tangled in their steps. You see women with lipstick grotesquely smeared across their faces, fallen on the curb. [...] If you travel a little farther downtown, you see things that were once men sleeping in doorways, huddled around trashcan fires, their filthy rags they wear hardly enough to cover them, begging nickels from strangers, with no place to go, no family that will recognise them.

This isn't far from the language Bob Dylan often preached from the stage in his Jesus times. Along with the waves of self-righteousness and scorn, there was a sense of play and glee, far more in the sermons, really, than in the songs. As in Albuquerque, in December 1979, as he was just rolling his gospel train onto the track: 'I told you the times they are a changin' and they did. I said the answer was blowin' in the wind and it was. I'm telling you now that Jesus is coming back, and He is!' Or as Todd Haynes boiled down a year of Dylan's own stage preaching in his multi-character Bob Dylan film, the 2007 *I'm Not There*, in this case the sixties folk hero Jack Rollins, for twenty years living as Pastor John in his church near Stockton, in the nowhere of California's Central Valley, speaking to his working-class congregation, black and Latino and white, a small crowd on folding chairs, the stains of alcohol and drugs in their faces, with

Christian Bale's pastor in a bad perm and a pastel blue leisure suit, with musicians and singers behind him, leading up to a shockingly convincing performance of Dylan's truest, most classical gospel song, 'Pressing On,' with Jon Doe's soundtrack voice coming out of his mouth.

*

Well I'm pressing on
Yes, I'm pressing on
Well I'm pressing on
To the higher calling of my Lord.
Many try to stop me, shake me up in my mind,
Say, "Prove to me that He is Lord, show me a sign."
What kind of sign they need when it all come from within,
When what's lost has been found, what's to come has already been?

*

But just before that there's a sermon. Bale's Jack Rollins delivers it as if he's given it to himself a thousand times before.

*

Now, I've never lied to you. I never told you who to vote for, or to follow anybody—back then, when I was selling records. What I didn't know is that it didn't matter what kind of music you played. It didn't matter what kind of music I was playing. Folk. Pop. Rock and roll. All rolled up in the devil's pocket—I'm not talking about a devil with a pitchfork and horns. I'm talking about a spiritual devil. At the midnight hour! And he's got to be overcome. And we, here in America, we shall overcome. Because this is America's holy gift! What greater honour for a nation than to speak for God? For some say that the war to end all wars has already begun, right now, in the Middle East, where it is prophesied the weak will fall and Jesus will set up his kingdom in Jerusalem. So why should we worry when we're already free! Right here, right now! And why are you free? You're free because Jesus paid for you to be. That's why you're free! Free to seek the higher calling of the Lord. Now pick up your bed—and walk.

*

That's the world Lucy Sante travels through. Reading what she wrote, you might catch the high spirits of the work.

Lucy Sante's books include *Low Life* (Farrar, Straus & Giroux, 2003), *Kill All Your Darlings* (Verse Chorus Press, 2007), *The Other Paris* (Farrar, Straus & Giroux, 2015), *Maybe the People Would Be the Times* (Verse Chorus Press, 2020), and the memoir, *I Heard Her Call My Name* (Heinemann, 2024).

Greil Marcus is the author of *Lipstick Traces: A Secret History of the Twentieth Century* (Harvard University Press, 1989). He contributed an introduction to the New York Review Books edition of Constance Rourke's 1931 *American Humour: A Study of the National Character*. He was born in San Francisco and lives in Oakland.

Six Sermons for Bob Dylan
Lucy Sante

Lucy Sante, © 2024; Greil Marcus, © 2024.

Sante's *Six Sermons* was first published in the United Kingdom by Tenement Press, 2024, edited by Dominic J. Jaeckle, and designed and typeset by Traven T. Croves (Matthew Stuart & Andrew Walsh-Lister).

Edited versions of these sermons are delivered by Michael Shannon, as directed by Jennifer Lebeau, on the DVD included in the deluxe edition of Bob Dylan's *Trouble No More: The Bootleg Series Vol. 13—1979–1981* (2017). Lebeau's *Trouble No More* was broadcast thereafter in the UK on the BBC as an entry in the station's *Arena* series, 2018. *Six Sermons* was published by special arrangement with Dylan's management. Marcus's afterword, 'Now pick up your bed—and walk,' was a special commission for this publication.

The rights of Lucy Sante and Greil Marcus to be identified as authors of this work have been asserted in accordance with Section 77 of the Copyright, Designs and Patents Act 1988. All efforts to identify copyright and secure permissions have been pursued where necessary and possible; fair dealing of works is listed in Section 30a, Schedule 2 (2a) of the Copyright, Designs and Patents Act 1988.

ILLUSTRATIONS—Ebenezer Baptist Church (407 Auburn Avenue, Atlanta, GA, 30312), *From afar* (p.11) / *Curb side* (p.17), care of the Atlanta History Center (atlantahistorycenter.com). The portrait of Rev. Matthew G. Carter, Dr. Martin Luther King, Jr., and Rev. Deual C. Rice (p.15) at the Union Baptist Church of Montclair (12–14 Midland Avenue, Montclair, NJ, 07042), 1966, is excerpted from a newspaper clipping by way of the church's archive. The bill poster (p.63) advertising the Piney Grove and Rockdale Park appearances of Rev. J.M. Gates ('first and third Sundays,' Piney Grove, Buck Head, Atlanta, GA, and 'second and fourth Sundays,' Mt. Calvary Baptist Church, Rockdale Park, Atlanta, GA, *date unknown*) is borrowed from findagrave.com.

Stickered editions carry an adornment; a photograph by Jet Lowe of a pulpit view of the Ebenzer Baptist Church: 'INTERIOR, VIEW FROM BEHIND PULPIT, LOOKING TOWARD BALCONY —Martin Luther King, Jr. National Historic Site, Ebenezer Baptist Church, 407 Auburn Avenue Northeast, Atlanta, Fulton County, GA' (Historic American Buildings Survey), retrieved from the Library of Congress, 2024; see also, p.7. The photographic scans included on pp.28, 33, 34, 40, 45, 46, 51, 52, 57, and 58 appear courtesy of Lucy Sante.

No part of this publication may be reproduced, stored in a retrieval system, or transmitted in any form or by any means electronic, mechanical, photocopying, recording or otherwise without prior permission in writing from Tenement Press.

A CIP record for this publication is available from the British Library.

Tenement 15, MMXXIV
ISBN 978-1-917304-01-6

Printed and bound by Lulu.
Typeset in Arnhem Pro Blond.

Tenement Press is an occasional publisher of esoteric;
experimental;
accidental;
and interdisciplinary literatures.

www.tenementpress.com
editors@tenementpress.com

Printed and bound by CPI Group (UK) Ltd, Croydon, CR0 4YY
29/04/2025
01855895-0002